A Halal Novel For Muslim Women

Love Scripts

Getting Through To Him

By Naielah Ackbarali
Muslima Coaching

Table of Contents

Chapter One:

The Forgotten Date Night

Sarah looked up at the wall clock again. She watched as the small clock hand gracefully moved towards the number eight.

Late again, she thought to herself.

He said that he was going to be home at six tonight. Sarah bit her lower lip as she reflected quietly.

Maybe he forgot about our date night. I assumed he would just remember.

She let out a loud sigh. It was pointless. Her husband was always forgetting. A feeling of increased tension immediately crept on to her shoulders at the thought of her husband's irresponsible memory record.

Geez, how hard is it to send a reminder email to himself? Surely there must be a way for him to stop his bad ways. Can't he just get his act together? He should just...

She suddenly paused. She remembered their marriage counselor, Mrs. Bradley, saying something about not trying to change the other person – that it was a fundamental key to forming a great relationship. She tried to rack her brain for the exact piece of advice.

Oh, this is hopeless! She doesn't know my husband. How can you not try to change someone when they need to change?

The sound of a car door slamming interrupted her thoughts. *He's home!*

She jumped up and rushed to the front door. She passed by a full-length mirror and caught a quick glimpse of her outfit: his favorite hijab along with his mother's specially chosen top from Pakistan. Not her personal choice but she was willing to do anything to make this marriage work after having two kids.

And deep down inside, she knew that she wasn't just trying for the kids' sake. She was also tired of feeling lonely in her marriage and longed for a better friendship with her husband.

Sarah heard her husband, Ahmad, stick the key in the door and fumble around to open it. She waited anxiously as he calmly opened the door and walked inside the house.

"Assalamu alaykum," he said in a deep voice. His gaze set upon her. He looked her up and down, and said nothing.

"wa alaykum assalam," she replied, opening her arms wider so that he would notice her outfit.

"I'm hungry. What's for dinner?" he moaned.

"Nothing. I haven't cooked. We were supposed to have a date night tonight. It's the third Friday of the month today, remember?" she quickly replied, trying to hide any hint of disappointment in her tone.

"Oh man. Has the time flown that fast? I completely forgot. I've been at the office all day trying to crack some new website codes for that big deal I was telling you about. It's been a long day. Should we order in at that halal joint?"

Sarah flinched. She was sick of being at home. Leaving her career as a doctor to homeschool and raise her two children was a decision that she consciously made for herself, but it definitely had its consequences. Couldn't he understand the sacrifices she was making? All she was asking for was to spare one night a month!

"Well, I thought we should go out," she began.

"Yeah but I'm tired," Ahmad retorted.

"Well, so am I, but maybe if we went to the restaurant we would feel better. You know, get some fresh air and experience a new atmosphere," she replied, hoping to convince him that he needed to go out as much as she did.

"I can't be bothered. I'm happy staying at home. Hey, how did Abdullah do on his exam?"

Sarah lowered her shoulders. It seemed like all they ever talked about were the kids.

"Yeah fine," she muttered, crossing her arms over her chest.

"Great," Ahmad replied, oblivious to her change in demeanor. "So what did you decide for dinner? Ordering may just be the easy thing for everyone."

"Yeah whatever," she muttered again.

"Okay let's get the usual then. We can spend the night catching up. We don't need a restaurant to do that for us," Ahmad said brightly.

Sarah sighed, caught between her feelings of sadness and disappointment. "Yeah, okay. Sure, whatever you want." She turned away and slowly walked towards the kitchen in defeat.

Eight years gone and two kids later, this was their everyday marriage. Even though she was unhappy, Sarah knew divorce wasn't an option for her. She always wanted to marry and fall in love, but it seemed like her husband was clueless about how to keep the romance alive.

Her mind wandered as she quietly reminisced about her marriage. The first year was easy. Married life was literally a breeze. She was sure that Ahmad and her would lead a promising relationship together.

They were both university educated, career-driven individuals. She studied to be a pediatrician and continued to work the first four years of their marriage, but when their second child came into the picture, things began to change.

She couldn't handle a full-time job any longer. It wasn't about putting in the hours; she could easily do that. But it was managing the guilt that she felt whenever she handed her son, Abdullah, and her daughter, Yasmine, over to her in-laws for babysitting. It didn't seem right that they were raising her children, especially during these crucial years.

Being at work was double torture. She always felt a stab of pain when her little patients smiled happily at their mothers who were dutifully by their sides.

After much deliberation, Sarah made the difficult choice to leave her career and dedicate herself to her family as a full-time stay-at-home mother. This was a hard decision for her, but she didn't regret it, not all the time at least.

Ahmad was supportive. He came from a traditional Pakistani background where the males were generally the main breadwinners, but he liked that

Sarah worked, and it was what initially attracted him to her.

He wanted an educated woman who could contribute to the family welfare. Yet, after the birth of Yasmine, he secretly desired for a better home life for his children. When Sarah mentioned that she was considering leaving her job to stay at home, he whole-heartedly agreed and promised to take on the role of the sole provider.

Sarah was definitely happy with spending more time with her children, but the dynamic in her relationship transformed with her husband in the process. Her annoyance at his flaws grew now that she had the time to pay attention to them, and her ability to be patient and control her irritation when he let her down was at an all-time low. Managing two children was hard enough as it was, and she didn't have the willpower to raise her husband along with them.

Ahmad followed her into the kitchen.

"Where's the menu? What do you want to order?"

"Whatever. I don't care," Sarah said, avoiding his eyes.

"What's with you? Just tell me what you want."

To go to the restaurant, she thought to herself.

"Nothing. Whatever. I'm fine. I'm not hungry anymore," she said stubbornly, half-hoping that he could read her mind.

Ahmad slammed the menu on the table. "You're going through one of those moods again! It's so annoying. You're ruining our night."

Sarah felt her cheeks get hot as her anger rose. "Me?!" she gasped. "You're the one who forgot about tonight. AGAIN!" she stressed the last word in a sarcastic tone.

Ahmad could barely contain himself. "I've been working all day. How am I supposed to remember some stupid date night with all the responsibilities I have? What do you have to worry about when you're at home all day – which detergent to use for the laundry?"

That was it. Forget the marriage counselor. Sarah exploded.

"It has nothing to do with your work responsibilities. When I was working, I could remember the kids' needs, a date night, and a lot more than that. My job was more stressful than yours. All you do is write website codes. Maybe if you applied yourself better, you could write a memo to yourself and be less forgetful."

Ahmad angrily pushed his chair back and stormed out of the kitchen, slamming the door harshly behind him.

"I'm just trying to help!" Sarah yelled out behind him. She felt the urge to cry but held back her tears with every ounce of strength possible.

Chapter Two:

The Pity Party

"**G**eez, how insensitive! How do you put up with it?" Sarah's younger sister, Iman, exclaimed.

Sarah flipped her long, black hair back and switched her cell phone to her other ear. She took a deep breath. Even though Iman was single, it felt overly comforting to hear someone's support.

"Well, I guess he's stressed out," Sarah added shyly, believing it was fair to say something in her husband's defense.

"Still! It's unacceptable. You're just as stressed. Surely he can't think that taking care of two children is easy, especially with a hyperactive son like Abdullah."

Sarah smiled at her sister's comment. Abdullah was definitely a handful but that's what made him so loveable.

"I know…" Sarah's voice drifted. She wasn't sure what to say. It was pretty unfair.

"If I were you, I'd give him a piece of my mind!" Iman snorted.

Sarah tilted her head to the side, debating whether that was necessary.

"I did tell him that I was stressed too and if he would just get more organized, these things wouldn't happen."

"Definitely," Iman chimed in, "It doesn't take that much effort to schedule in a reminder these days."

"That's exactly what I was thinking," Sarah said in a quivering voice, holding back her tears. "Do you think he loves me? I mean, why doesn't he put more effort into our relationship? It's me that had to find Mrs. Bradley and drag him to the first appointment."

"This is precisely why I'm not marrying a Pakistani! My dream guy is definitely a convert. Look at all the men in our family. They just expect their wives to wait hand and foot on them. I've never heard any of them say a thank you to their wives! Sometimes men can be selfish and self-centered, even dad..."

"Iman..." Sarah protested. "Don't go there. It's the last thing I want to hear about."

"Well it's true," Iman huffed. She quickly changed the subject.

"Look at what's happened to you Sarah," Iman added in a soft voice. "You were the star of the family, the first woman to graduate from university and become a doctor. Now you're just a housewife. I'm worried about you. I miss my sister, the champion woman that I know her to be."

Sarah silently listened to her sister's words. She knew Iman was right but she was torn. She loved her kids and leaving her job to take care of them was the best decision she made, but it was her husband's unsupportive behavior that was the problem. It was difficult to get through to him, to make him understand what she was experiencing in her life, and convincing him to help her out.

"I just don't know what to do. He doesn't talk much and when I try to prompt him, he's short with me. I just want him to open up to me. Ugh, it's so frustrating!" Sarah leaned back in her chair.

"Well that's why mom is always complaining about dad. He just won't compromise. Things have to be his way. She feels like he never considers her preferences, and it's only when she nags him to death that he yields.

"When we were younger, I didn't really notice what was happening between the two of them, but now that I'm in my twenties, I can see things for what they are. I'm surprised they are still together after forty years with the way dad acts.

"It's also why I am thinking of not marrying. When I hear that you're going through the same thing, it makes me think that all men are the same. Why bother!"

"There are benefits to being married, Iman," Sarah noted.

"Like what?" Iman challenged. "All I see is that you gave up everything to please your husband and he hasn't lived up to his side of the bargain."

"Well, for one, you can't have your own kids without getting married."

"Okay so I won't have kids. There are so many in the world anyway. Why not help those that are having a hard time, like orphans? That seems more pleasing to Allah. Think about it Sarah. I can contribute my time towards charity and make a bigger impact on the world. I'm not going to spend all this time studying just to become a stay-at-home mom," Iman insisted.

"Whatever Iman," Sarah said, rolling her eyes. "Superwoman is for the movies, not real life. I have to run. Talk to you later inshaAllah."

Sarah knew that her sister was still immature and inexperienced with love. She believed that at every woman's core, her deepest desire was to fall in love, share her life with someone, have kids, grow old, and live happily-ever-after.

Iman was temporarily blinded by the assortment of opportunities in front of her, but she would eventually reach the same realization that Sarah did: a stressful career is not worth it and married life is. She just didn't know how to get Ahmad to feel the same way about their marriage.

Sarah pressed her back comfortably into the chair, reflecting further. She replayed the scene with Ahmad over and over in her head, analyzing it from every angle possible. She couldn't see where it all went wrong and why he would suddenly turn angry over certain things she said. They couldn't relate to each other outside of the children's interests.

Iman's words echoed in her mind. *Sometimes men can be selfish and self-centered, even dad…*

Sarah looked outside the window, chewing on Iman's comment. Her father was a kind man, but he definitely had his moments of challenging behavior. She remembered finding her parents in a heated argument when she was ten years old returning home from school one day.

Her father was speaking in a raised voice, telling her mother that he was going to put his foot down with her. She recalled his fists shaking in the air and the intensity of his facial expression.

Her mother was not the least bit intimidated. She stood glaring back at him, as if he was a little child who needed disciplining. "Just save some money on the side!" her mother protested. "The children need savings to go to university! Can't you find a better job and make more money?"

Sarah's dad let out a cry of frustration, turned around, and stormed off. Her parents didn't talk to each other for a few days after that, but things eventually returned to normal. Sarah never mentioned what she saw to anyone, but that memory made a strong impression on her.

She would often feel upset at her father for how he treated her mother. It was a heaviness that she carried with her and still felt until this day. She couldn't make sense of his moods. They appeared completely unjustifiable to her. Ahmad was similar to her father in this regard.

Sarah wondered if their marriage would also be like her parent's own forty years down the line. She prayed that it would be different, but it certainly seemed to be heading down the same path. And after speaking with Iman, she felt doubly sorry for her situation.

Chapter Three:

Mr. Macho Uncut

Ahmad ran his fingers through his soaked hair. His entire body was drenched in sweat and his muscles were aching from all the exertion.

This feels so good – just what I needed after all that commotion.

He positioned his body for another round of kettlebell swings. He looked at his form out of the corner of his eye in the wall-to-wall gym mirror. It was perfect and ready for another intense workout.

All he needed was something to make him feel successful again and an extreme exercise routine always did the trick. The high of challenging his body gave him an extra boost, and when he pushed himself to beat his last record, it provided an unexplainable feeling of accomplishment – like he could win at anything.

He was driven to succeed. His father pressed him since he was ten years old to aim high and work for every penny he earned. Crying for help was not an option. His dad taught him to push himself hard, and when that wasn't good enough, the solution was to push himself even more.

In general, he was good at whatever he put his mind to and he personally craved to achieve promising results. He didn't always have to be on top, but he needed to feel successful at whatever he decided to invest his energy and time into. Most people saw his good work ethic and praised his attempts to do well for himself – except his wife.

What's up with her? She's never satisfied, always complaining about something or in one of her moods.

Ahmad felt his stress levels lowering as he swung the kettlebell. He was frustrated with his marriage, but he didn't know how to change things. He found himself working extra hours or hanging out at the gym more frequently because he couldn't stand going home and being around Sarah's negative vibe.

It wasn't always like this. He put his kettlebell down to take a water break.

When he first married Sarah, his heart was on his sleeve. It was exciting to select his partner for life. He wanted to fall in love, provide for his wife, grow old together, and be religious partners. He liked Sarah's unique ambition and her sharp mind. It's why he married her.

After giving birth to their second child, Sarah changed. She was no longer fun to be around. She complained a lot about taking care of the children along with the stress of her job. When she finally decided to stop working, Ahmad was pleased. He thought that this would be the answer to her unhappiness.

But it wasn't – it was merely the beginning. Even though he was working more hours to support them, Sarah never seemed satisfied with the choices that he was making. She chastised him for any little mistake he made.

He did forget about a few key appointments, like their five-year anniversary, but it was only because he was pushing himself at work. He didn't have a choice. It was his responsibility to provide and he took it seriously. He couldn't bear the thought of letting his family down and he wanted to give them whatever he could afford.

He knew that Sarah was making sacrifices too, and he appreciated her dedication towards raising the children, but he hoped that she would notice his dedication towards being the sole provider. His job wasn't easy and he felt the pressure to perform at work. His career field was getting more competitive and impressing his boss was tough.

All he wanted was someone who would acknowledge him and admire him, as well as appreciate his efforts. He needed to feel like he was coming home to his biggest fan, not another uptight boss. Her negativity and disapproving looks drove him away. He couldn't stand her attitude anymore but he didn't know how to tell her what he was really thinking without blowing up. She never asked anyway. Maybe she didn't care.

One thing was for sure. He cared about her deeply, and he wanted things to be different for the two of them, but it was beyond him how things could possibly change for the better.

***

Sarah lay in bed waiting for Ahmad to return home. She couldn't sleep knowing that he was away from her. She did worry about him.

She loved him too, but it was a strange type of love. It wasn't what she expected love for a husband to be like. It was an unusual sensation of longing to stay with someone, but it was constantly being polluted with an unsettling feeling of disappointment and intrusive doubts.

She heard Ahmad pull up to the driveway and the car engine turn off. She waited as he slowly made his way up the stairs and gently opened the bedroom door. She said nothing to him and remained motionless as he undressed and slipped into bed.

She could smell the sweat on him. He was quite stinky.

"Don't you want to take a shower?" she suggested, breaking the silence.

"No," he replied with his back turned to her.

"How can you go to sleep like that? It's gross." she added, hoping that he would agree.

"I'll just sleep on the couch if it bothers you so much. I've got to get to work early tomorrow and I don't want to think about it right now." He rose to leave.

Sarah didn't want him to go, but she couldn't find the words to express how she felt. She wished that he would understand her better. She needed him to be more attentive to her desires – to be able to read her.

"I called Mrs. Bradley for an appointment tomorrow," she blurted out. She wanted him to know that she was trying to make things work. She only desired to talk about their relationship for the sake of improving it. She hoped that he would do the same.

Ahmad let out a grunt. He hated going to those sessions. They were absolute torture. They often ended with him being blamed for their marriage problems.

"Can we talk about this later? I've got work tomorrow." He hurried out of bed and left her stranded in the bedroom.

Sarah felt a stab of pain in her heart. She was lonely. She turned her face towards the *qibla* and prayed that Allah would come to her aid. Saving her marriage seemed to be doomed, but hopefully the next counseling appointment would create an unforgettable opening.

Chapter Four:

The Final Session

Ahmad smoothly steered the car into an empty parking space. Sarah opened the passenger door and placed her two feet flat on the road. She glanced up at the sky, praying that today would be different.

The drive to Mrs. Bradley's was awkward. Ahmad hardly said anything to her. It made her overly anxious. She wondered what he was thinking. Did he love her as much as she loved him?

She looked ahead and noticed that Ahmad had already walked towards Mrs. Bradley's office. She jumped out of the car, slammed the door, and rushed to catch up with him.

Mrs. Bradley invited them in and signaled that they should take their usual places. Ahmad plopped himself down on the leather chair, leaned back, with his legs wide open like he was watching a football game. Sarah sat on the leather chair directly facing him, crossed her legs, and straightened her back.

The sunset light peeped through the office window and shone onto Mrs. Bradley's silver hair, creating a rainbow of orange and red hues on her face.

She shuffled some papers on her desk, cleared her throat, and looked at Ahmad, then at Sarah.

"So, what's on your minds? How was your date night?" she inquired.

Ahmad slumped further into his chair. Sarah winced at his slight movement and turned to Mrs. Bradley.

"Well, we didn't have a date night because Ahmad forgot about it." Sarah revealed.

Mrs. Bradley raised her eyebrows in surprise. She knew Ahmad had a tendency to forget about his appointments, but this was uncalled for considering the state of their marriage.

"Ahmad?" Mrs. Bradley asked, looking for an explanation.

Ahmad shrugged his shoulders. Sarah's blood began to boil.

"Don't you have anything to say?" Sarah poked at him. She couldn't stand his nonchalant attitude towards their relationship.

"Yes." Ahmad said. He turned to Mrs. Bradley, "How do I get Sarah to stop bothering me about these date nights when I'm stressed out at work?"

Mrs. Bradley braced herself. She knew what was coming: World War III.

"Bothering *you*?" Sarah coldly asked. "We wouldn't be here if you learned how to be more organized."

"Maybe if you got off my back then I could breathe better and I wouldn't need to become more organized." Ahmad shot back.

Sarah froze. Ahmad's comment stung. He never spoke to her like that before; things were getting worse. He was getting worse. How was she going to save their relationship?

She felt the urge to cry but held back her tears. She was too strong to let him win. Revenge seemed sweeter. She opened her mouth to fight back. She was determined to prove her point.

"If you would act more responsibly then I wouldn't have to waste my breath!" Sarah remarked, trying to sound objective.

"You're wasting your time by complaining all the time. It doesn't do us any good."

"Don't blame me. It's not my fault we're coming to these sessions. I'm only trying to help. We can't keep heading in this direction. The children are suffering the most. Remember when you forgot about Abdullah's pool party? He was crushed."

"Are you still complaining about that? Geez, it happened six months ago. I've done so much to make up for it. Get over it!" Ahmad exclaimed.

"Can't you admit when you're wrong? You're still not spending time with them! I'm not going to let my children down the way you do. You're so busy caught up in your career and personal ambitions that the kids don't even know their father anymore. It's like they're growing up without a dad."

Ahmad angrily glared at Sarah. The children's well-being was a sore spot for him. He was ready to up the ante and wage a full-blown war on her. Just as he was about to give his battle cry, Mrs. Bradley interrupted them.

"Stop it you two. You're attacking each other," she said in an authoritative tone.

Mrs. Bradley paused to check that they were listening to her and then continued in a gentle voice, "Take a deep breath, face each other, and say the truth with compassion."

Sarah stared at the floor, inhaled deeply, and exhaled twice as long. She recognized this familiar drill. Expressing her angry feelings came easily to her and sometimes she didn't know when to stop. She appreciated that Mrs. Bradley called the shots and regulated their arguments. She honestly felt that they would go on forever if it wasn't for her intervention.

Sarah raised her head to look at Ahmad but he was avoiding her gaze. She gritted her teeth and forced herself to say in the most compassionate voice possible:

"Ahmad, you forgot about our date night and our marriage is suffering because of your irresponsibility. It makes me extremely upset at you. If you want us to have a good marriage, you must change."

She felt instant relief. The truth had been spoken. All that needed to happen was for Ahmad to admit to his wrong. She paused and hoped for a positive response.

Ahmad looked around the office like a caged animal looking for an escape route. He stared at Mrs. Bradley for a few seconds and then at Sarah and then at Mrs. Bradley again. His right leg bounced up and down to an angry beat. He was ready to explode of rage.

He jumped up and said in a booming voice, "Mrs. Bradley, with all due respect, I know that you're trying to help us but it's not working for me. I can't come back here. This is our final session. Goodbye."

Sarah gasped in shock. Ahmad turned his back on both of them, pushed open the door, and dashed out of Mrs. Bradley's office like a criminal on the loose.

Chapter Five:

Glad Tidings

The ride home was miserable. Ahmad wouldn't even look at Sarah. He kept his eyes intensely fixed on the road ahead with his hands tightly gripped on the steering wheel. His lips were drawn across his face in a strict line and he leaned forward in his seat like he was in a bumper car, ready to ram something.

Sarah was smart enough to know that she couldn't say anything when he was like this. She had seen Ahmad get into these types of moods before. When she described them to Mrs. Bradley, she mentioned that Ahmad was stonewalling. It was a common way that men dealt with their anger in conflict.

Sarah couldn't get her head around the psychological concept. She half believed it. She honestly felt Ahmad had unresolved anger issues. She concluded that he didn't know how to deal with differences of opinion and became furious if anyone challenged his way. It seemed selfish. Maybe Iman was right about men.

She closed her eyes, sinking deeper into her thoughts. She wanted to be able to speak openly with Ahmad about their relationship. His inability to admit to any wrong that he committed was killing their connection. It was ridiculous that he was willing to throw eight years of marriage down the drain for the sake of his ego.

Ring. Ring.

Ahmad reached over for his cell phone and answered.

"Assalamu alaykum." The car went silent for a few seconds as Ahmad listened to the caller speak.

"Oh, that's great man! Congratulations!" His face beamed with a huge smile. He became a different person in an instant. "Yeah. Yeah…Okay we'll stop by tomorrow inshaAllah."

Ahmad hung up the phone and returned his gaze back to the road. He was more relaxed than before.

"Who was it?" Sarah asked curiously, assuming that it was safe to speak now.

"It was Muhammad. Aisha just had a baby girl." He replied excitedly, grinning from ear to ear.

Muhammad was Ahmad's eldest brother. They weren't as close as Sarah was to Iman, but they had a good relationship with each other. Aisha was Muhammad's wife, a Syrian sister who he married ten years ago. They were the only multicultural couple in Ahmad's family. This was their third child but their first baby girl.

"Oh, Abdullah and Yasmine are going to be so excited to find out they have a new playmate." Sarah replied, hoping Ahmad would loosen up more. Things appeared to go well when the kids' names were mentioned.

Ahmad nodded proudly with a huge smile. His eyes gleamed with joy. He loved children.

"We'll visit them tomorrow inshaAllah." Ahmad added. "Abdullah and Yasmine will definitely want to play with the baby once we tell them."

Sarah smiled weakly. She didn't feel like smiling but she knew that it would be rude if she didn't. It was always a joyous occasion when another Muslim entered the world.

"Sure inshaAllah. Tomorrow is Saturday. The kids will be off from homeschooling. It's perfect. Allah is the best of planners."

Ahmad leaned back in his seat. He looked over at Sarah reassuringly and smiled. It was if the entire scene that occurred at Mrs. Bradley's was forgotten.

Chapter Six:

The Opening

Abdullah burst through the front door, barely able to contain his excitement. Sarah hardly noticed his hyperactive nature anymore, but Ahmad felt slightly embarrassed by his son's wild behavior.

"Me! Me! I get to hold the baby first!" Abdullah said, jumping up and down.

Muhammad came out of the bedroom with a big smile on his face.

"Assalamu alaykum little guy! How much sugar did you eat today?" he joked while ruffling Abdullah's hair.

"Just one lollipop and a cookie," Abdullah replied quickly, speaking at the speed of a hundred words a minute.

Muhammad raised his right eyebrow. "Is that all? Are you sure?"

Abdullah shook his head up and down, and then side to side, and then up and down again. Muhammad and Ahmad laughed.

"Where's the baby?" Abdullah asked eagerly.

"She's sleeping but you can go in with your mother and see her." Muhammad suggested.

"Moooommmmmmmmm!!!" Abdullah screamed.

"Calm down Abdullah," Sarah ordered while walking through the front door holding Yasmine's hand.

"Assalamu alaykum Muhammad. Congratulations. May Allah bless all your children inshaAllah."

"Jazak Allah khayran, and yours too. You can go in and see Aisha. She's resting with the baby."

Sarah nodded and opened the bedroom door. Aisha was sitting up in bed, holding the newborn baby to her chest. She rocked her back and forth, peering down at her like she had a golden treasure in her hands.

Aisha's appearance was lovely. She looked happy and refreshed. Her brown, wavy hair was tied back in a neat ponytail and her hazel eyes sparkled with love. She raised her head as Sarah walked into the room.

"Assalamu alaykum Sarah," Aisha said in a hushed voice, indicating that the baby was still napping.

"wa alaykum assalam Aisha. Congratulations. MashaAllah we are so happy for you."

Abdullah's face lit up when he saw the baby.

"Can I hold her please, Khaltu?" he asked politely.

"She's sleeping now. Why don't you climb into bed and you can watch her with me?"

Abdullah accepted the invitation, and it wasn't long before he was snuggled next to Aisha, staring down at her baby with wide eyes. He touched her little arm and giggled.

Yasmine held out a gift bag. "Khaltu, this is for you."

"Oh, thank you Yasmine. How sweet! You shouldn't have!"

Aisha grinned. "So, who does she look like? Me or Uncle Muhammad?"

Abdullah looked confused. He wasn't sure how to tell.

"Both!" he exclaimed.

Aisha and Sarah laughed together.

Sarah had never really bonded with her sister-in-law. They only saw each other at family gatherings and births. They were acquaintances more than they were friends.

"So how did the birth go?" Sarah inquired. "InshaAllah it was easy and without difficulty."

"AlhamduliLlah," Aisha said, stressing the Arabic letters with her Damascene accent. "By Allah's favor, it was the easiest birth I've ever had." She smiled warmly, continuing to rock the baby in a slow rhythmic fashion.

"The pregnancy was a bit challenging but the birth was simple," she clarified. "Actually, I can't complain because Muhammad has been a big help. He has been so considerate and caring. I don't know what I'd do without him." Aisha smiled peacefully.

Sarah's heart ached. How could the two brothers act so differently? Maybe she should tell Muhammad to talk to his brother and teach him how to be a better husband.

"Oh...ugh...That's nice." Sarah was lost for words.

"We're so lucky to be married to these guys, aren't we? They treat us like queens mashaAllah." Aisha commented innocently.

Sarah slowly swallowed a lump in her throat.

"Mmmm..." Sarah managed to mumble a bit unnaturally.

"Mom, can I go play outside?" Abdullah interrupted anxiously. He was tired of observing the baby.

"Yes, sure. Take Yasmine with you."

"Okay!!!" Abdullah grabbed Yasmine's hand and raced out of the bedroom, slamming the bedroom door behind him.

The baby's eyes opened suddenly and she began to cry.

"Oh, I'm sorry," Sarah said, blushing from shyness.

"It's fine. Don't worry." Aisha said coolly, well-aware of Abdullah's active nature.

Sarah watched as Aisha placed the baby against her breast and left her to suckle. She wondered what made her relationship with Muhammad so different from her own with Ahmad. She was initially too ashamed to ask, but curiosity overcame her.

"So...how do you get Muhammad to do things for you?" Sarah inquired nervously while attempting to sound normal.

Aisha was not so easily fooled. She knew that there was more to Sarah's question but she played along, not wanting to embarrass her guest.

A year ago, she haphazardly caught Sarah and Ahmad fighting with each other in her mother-in-law's kitchen. Muhammad also told her that the two were having difficulties and were seeing Mrs. Bradley for the past few months.

Aisha thoughtfully reflected. As she tilted her head to the side, her ponytail fell onto her shoulder. She pressed her full lips together and carefully opened her mouth.

"To be honest, I think I try to not make Muhammad feel bad when he doesn't live up to my expectations."

Sarah took a few moments to digest her comment. This was unknown territory for her. She had received a lot of marriage advice from her friends and professionals, but it always revolved around being patient or speaking up for yourself. Although these concepts made sense in principle, she never understood how to strike a balance between the two.

"What do you mean?" Sarah pushed further. "How could a wife make her husband feel bad?"

Aisha stared intensely into Sarah's eyes. She was assessing if Sarah was ready to hear the truth – what was greatly contributing to her marriage problems.

"By criticizing instead of helping," Aisha remarked. She paused briefly and watched Sarah's reaction. Sarah's face was dressed with confusion. Aisha felt it was safe to continue with her explanation.

"When things don't happen the way we're expecting, we can either waste our time blaming our husbands and criticizing them, or we can help them to become better people and teach them how to take care of us. This is why we must constantly check our intentions and question our expectations.

"Expectations set us up to feel disappointment when maybe there is nothing really to be upset over. They also limit our mind's ability to accept our circumstances, deal with them, and look for a solution. When we're stuck on the idea that our husbands should only act and react a certain way, it can damage our marriages more than we may realize."

Sarah was startled by Aisha's response. Were her expectations of Ahmad impacting her marriage? Was she blaming and criticizing him? Was she also doing something to hurt their marriage? Up until this moment, she always assumed it was Ahmad's fault for their problems.

"Well how can someone not criticize the other person's actions when they're doing wrong?" Sarah said, playing devil's advocate. She wasn't fully convinced by Aisha's theory.

Aisha was completely prepared to tackle Sarah's rejection of her idea.

"By turning the criticism into conversation – by expressing your own personal need or preference to him, without pressuring him to feel the same way you do. Humans learn through example. You teach him how to treat you by the way that you treat him."

Sarah snorted. *This is stupid. How's talking about it going to change anything?* she wondered to herself. *I've tried that already and he doesn't listen.*

Aisha realized that she needed to give an example. She grew up amongst a tightknit Syrian family, and she knew plenty of female relatives who showed her how to successfully make a man do things for a woman.

"Men have a deep desire to be accepted, admired, and appreciated, Sarah. Criticism does the opposite. It sends the signal that you're not his number one fan. Many women make the mistake of thinking that the more they criticize, the sooner their husbands will wake up and be charged to do things for them, but it's like quicksand. Once you go there, your relationship keeps sinking and you can never pull yourself out of it. You sink. Your husband sinks. Your relationship sinks."

Sarah could relate very well to this analogy. She frequently felt like she was sinking. Her heart was definitely sinking.

"The words that you use daily with your husband will cultivate a certain type of culture within your relationship. When you water your marriage with unbound criticism, contempt, and control, weeds will quickly grow over and cover the open plain of your hearts.

"Yet, when you nurture your marital seed with loving words, encouragement, and praise, a beautiful rose bush will burst forth over the years of being together inshaAllah. Kindness is catching. If you encourage your husband to be his best, he will be, and not only that, it will bring out the best in you too inshaAllah."

Sarah's interest was piqued. She wanted to bring out the best in herself. She leaned forward in an effort to hear Aisha's hushed voice better.

"One of my sister's is married to an American convert. He grew up in a strict household and his father was quite rough with him. After my sister's second child, the two of them were getting into all types of arguments. They kept butting heads on how to discipline the kids. He wanted something very rigid, but in Syria, we're very balanced with how we treat children.

"It was easy for her to resort to criticism. She would tell him things like, 'You're a convert. You don't know how to raise Muslim children. You can't talk to them like that. It's not the way a father should be. Your way is wrong.'

"Despite her insistence, her comments would bounce off of his back. He wouldn't listen to her. Sometimes it seemed like he was purposely being stricter to spite her. Their arguments were intensifying and they were starting to erupt in front of the kids.

"She prayed a lot to Allah to change her situation. She realized that whatever she was doing wasn't working, but at the same time, she couldn't stop complaining about her husband to my family."

In the back of her mind, Sarah knew that she was doing something similar whenever she confided in Iman.

"One day my mother told her that Allah would only hold her accountable for her actions, and not her husband's, so she should at least make sure that whatever she was doing was pleasing to Allah Most High.

"It was then that my aunty suggested that she try to acknowledge and appreciate his efforts as a father, and thereafter tell him what she preferred, as well as express why it was so important to her. See, if you want to get through to your husband, you have to make the effort to present your message in a tactful way – it's like delivering a love script."

A love script? Sarah thought to herself. She wasn't really good at writing.

"My sister was willing to try it. She made a lot of *du'a* that night for Allah to put blessing in her words. The next day, she asked her husband if he was free to talk about something that was important to her. He agreed to hear her out after dinner.

"She said to him, 'You are a great father and I know that you're trying hard. It means a lot to me that you care so much about our family. I really want our children to grow up in a household where they receive as much love as they do discipline. I need us to be a team together. It's all I want.'

"It was quite amazing what happened to her marriage afterwards. Her husband was initially hesitant but with time and the right words, the entire dynamic between them changed."

Sarah stared off into the distance. Her eyes landed on a large wooden dresser of drawers. The top of it was covered with makeup kits, a vanity mirror, and perfumes. Aisha must like to dress up.

Aisha noticed that Sarah was zoning out, but she wanted to finish her point. She didn't know if Sarah would be open to hear her ideas again.

"When a man believes that his wife accepts him for who he is, he feels emotionally safe. And when he's not interpreting his wife's comments as an attack, he's more willing to listen to her suggestions because it comes across as friendly advice, not overbearing orders."

Sarah's tolerance for Aisha's concepts was dwindling. She felt her face becoming hot out of annoyance. She knew that Aisha's understanding of men didn't apply to her situation. If only Ahmad would admit to his faults and change his behavior, then maybe she could accept him.

"When a man recognizes that he has a friend by his side, and not a mother or an enemy, he'll keep giving back to his wife because he is overly inspired to please her. That's how to get a man to do something for a woman. It's all about how she talks to him."

"Oh geez! Why does the woman have to do everything?" Sarah counter argued.

"It's not a gender thing, Sarah. It's an Islam thing. As a Muslim our goal must be to fill our scale pan with the best character that we can demonstrate towards our husbands for the sake of our eternal destination. The Prophet ﷺ said, 'Any woman who dies whilst her husband is pleased with her will enter Paradise.'

"It is from good character that a wife takes the means to please her husband to the best of her capability and to make her household a safe haven."

Aisha paused. She could sense that Sarah was starting to become defensive. Even though she was unsure of how receptive Sarah would be, she decided to take the chance of continuing.

"And it's not just for the husband's sake. The children need to grow up in a peaceful environment too. She will only gain the reward for trying to be a good wife. The more she makes her marriage a type of worship – a way to please Allah – the more she will remain enthusiastic about taking care of her husband's needs inshaAllah."

Sarah sat silently reflecting. She tried hard to make sense of Aisha's advice. It was overwhelming to think that she might be part of the problem, and even more off-putting to think that changing the way she spoke was a possible solution.

Aisha noticed her hesitation. "Come on Sarah, let's be honest. Women are at a stronger advantage than men in dropping love lines since they are naturally skilled in the areas of relationships and emotions.

"We are the keepers of our marriages. We are gifted with natural strengths that can make our marriages succeed. Just like we possess the charm to lighten up the room with our laughter, we can easily captivate our husbands with our sweet talk and praise.

"Some women want their husbands to robotically submit to their way, but it's not how a good marriage works. You have to help each other and not merely assert that you're in the right and think that you can say or do whatever you want without considering his feelings."

Sarah felt uncomfortable with Aisha's ideas. She couldn't bear to hear anymore.

She shifted her eyes to the baby, smiled politely, and quickly changed the subject.

Chapter Seven:

Willingness

"If they're wrong, they should submit," Iman passionately argued.

Sarah adjusted the volume on her earpiece so that she could hear Iman better. She reached for a package of spaghetti, placed it in her shopping cart, and pushed it forward.

"Mmmm..." she mumbled, still dazed after her conversation with Aisha.

"She's not a professional, Sarah. She's just a housewife. What would she know about men and marriages?"

Iman had a point, but Aisha must know something in order to have such a good marriage. She and Muhammad looked happy. Sarah couldn't remember when the last time was that she felt happy with Ahmad.

"And why is it always the woman's fault?" Iman aggressively questioned.

"She's not saying it's the woman's fault," Sarah hesitantly clarified. "I think she's suggesting that women have the capability to be the solution by speaking a certain way to their husbands – or something like that." She was still trying to face her own doubts about the concept as well.

"Ahmad's definitely not like his brother. I don't know how you could apply the same advice," Iman continued. "Does he even deserve to be admired and sweet talked?"

Sarah stopped moving. Her sister's words were cutting. Ahmad had his faults, but he was a good guy at heart. He just had unresolved anger issues from his childhood and it made him too sensitive to criticism. He needed to man up.

Sarah scanned the price of potatoes as her sister spoke.

"Maybe Muhammad treats her differently because she's not Pakistani. If he had married someone from his same culture, he would probably be just like his brother."

Sarah chewed her lip. She was starting to get annoyed at Iman's conclusions.

What benefit was she really gaining by talking to Iman about her marriage problems? It sometimes made her feel better knowing that someone felt sorry for her, but her sister's advice was more amateur than Aisha's 'unprofessional' background.

"Men today aren't what they used to be. Well, they weren't really good to start off with but now they're just getting worse," Iman persisted.

Sarah squinted. Iman's generalizations definitely reflected her immaturity. She was unmarried and clueless about men. Why did she think that she was some type of expert on them and relationships?

"When my dream guy comes, I'll tell him that he can't treat me that way. I won't settle for it."

Sarah was tired of listening to her sister's voice. "Iman, the Mahdi is going to come before your dream guy does," she snapped.

Iman's jaw dropped open. "Sarah?!" This was very much unlike her sister. Sarah barely used her witty nature against her.

"I have to go. I'm at the cashier's counter. Salam," Sarah said in a rush. She hung up her cell phone before Iman could respond, relieving herself of all the unwarranted advice.

Sarah tossed her groceries into the backseat of the car, jumped in, and headed home.

Her mind ached from all of the thinking that she was doing. She couldn't make sense of what Aisha said. It was contradictory to all the advice she had heard – that it took two to change a marriage. She hoped that talking to Iman would bring her clarity, but it only made matters worse. Now that Mrs.

Bradley was out of the picture, she would have to figure this one out on her own.

Sarah doubted whether Aisha's advice would work with her marriage. She sadly believed that it was too late to try such a tactic – to change the way she spoke. What was a love script anyway? It sounded like a cheesy line from a Disney movie.

She halted the car at the red light and drummed her fingers against the steering wheel. Ahmad wasn't a bad guy. He was the father of her children. Deep down, she loved him. She needed him. She wanted to have a good marriage. Her eyes began to well with tears. This time, she allowed them to freely flow.

What did it take to get through to him? Why was it so difficult? Could the two brothers be that different? But what if...what if they were really the same? What if Ahmad would respond the same way that Muhammad responded with Aisha?

She chewed her lower lip, caught up in her indecision. She wasn't sure how to deliver a 'love script.' She never saw any woman in her family saying love scripts, but then again, most of them had struggling marriages. She concluded a long time ago that many of her female relatives stayed in their marriages for the sake of their children and not because they loved their husbands.

As much as she did not want to admit it, she believed that her mother fell into that category. Her parents weren't continuously at odds with each other, but she could clearly tell that they weren't emotionally connected. Maybe this is why her mother was critical over her father, or was it the other way around – that her father distanced himself because her mother was too critical of him? She was at lost with how to analyze their relationship after speaking with Aisha.

All Sarah knew was that she longed to be different. She didn't want to get divorced, but she didn't want to stay married and in the same situation. Wasn't there any other way? She believed that she had tried everything to make things work with Ahmad…except a love script. Was this the answer to her prayers?

She always described herself as a determined, open-minded person. She was willing to try anything new and practical. People praised her for her down-to-earth and pragmatic personality.

Sarah sighed.

Maybe it didn't matter whose fault it was after all. Maybe what really mattered was the result that she received from doing whatever it took to make her marriage good.

She remembered Aisha's mother's words. *Allah would only hold her accountable for her actions, and not her husband's, so she should at least make sure that whatever she was doing was pleasing to Allah Most High.*

Sarah's heart jumped at the thought. These past years of struggling through her marriage had pulled her down spiritually. She rarely saw her marriage as a way to Allah, but in her heart, she knew that pleasing Allah was more important than pleasing herself. She couldn't continue like this – she didn't want to be in the same place anymore.

BEEP! BEEP! BEEP! BEEP!

Several horns blasted behind her, shaking Sarah out of her daze. The light had turned green and she was still stuck in the same spot, preventing everyone behind her from moving ahead. She wiped her tears away with the back of her palms.

She stepped on the pedal and started to progress forward – determined to head in a new direction for the sake of Allah.

She soon found herself pulling the car into her driveway. She opened the door and climbed out. She felt charged, strong, and energetic. Something great was about to happen; she could feel it in her bones. Her heart pounded with excitement.

It finally clicked. She couldn't control Ahmad but she could control herself – the way she talked and responded to him. Only one thing bothered her…

Was it really possible to change her marriage all on her own?

Chapter Eight:

The Kitchen Date

Ahmad sat at the kitchen table eating a chicken sandwich. He watched his children playing happily outside in the backyard. It brought him great joy to see them enjoying themselves. He took pride in being able to provide that opportunity for his children.

His childhood was quite different. There were happy times, but his father made it clear that Ahmad's purpose in life was to earn a living and be successful. He was constantly being pushed to try his best at school. His mother was his emotional backbone. She showed him love and support. If it wasn't for her, he would have caved in from his dad's pressure to perform a long time ago.

Because he was programmed to provide, it was difficult for Ahmad to feel like he was not successful at fulfilling the needs of his loved ones. He wanted to give his children a good, religious upbringing with plenty of opportunities at their hands. He was driven to offer them a wholesome life and a happy home. At a materialistic level, he knew that he was flying, but he still felt empty.

His mental process for analyzing life was similar to what he used at work when designing website codes. He was compelled to assess the outcome of each option before he would settle on which one to finally choose. He expended his energy and time towards carefully considering the pros and cons of each letter and number he wrote, except that Sarah's moods were the unpredictable factor that made it all turn wrong.

His marriage with Sarah was draining him. He couldn't win with her. He was inundated with doubts about staying or leaving the marriage now. He didn't want to argue anymore. He didn't want to feel like a loser. He didn't want to be pressured into always doing things her way. Was it worth it to be with her?

He hated the person he was becoming. He experienced angry emotions and frustration regularly at work, and returning home to a troubled environment and going to useless marriage counseling didn't make things better for him. He craved his own space – a place where he could relax.

He didn't know how to deal with Sarah. He was starting to feel unattracted to her. She had a pretty face and her body was more curvaceous after having two children, but that wasn't enough to satisfy him.

He longed for someone who would love him and appreciate him; someone who would ease his mind away from his stress at work and make him feel like a winner at home.

Even if he was forced to open up to her, he couldn't bring himself to trust Sarah with his deepest thoughts. All the criticism demotivated him from even trying to share his life with her. He never knew if what he was saying would be used against him later on in another conversation or met with half-hearted enthusiasm. It was demotivating and draining to be around her, especially when she was in one of her moods.

He just wanted to be seen and heard for who he was as a human being. He wanted to be understood for the values that defined him and drove his passions. He wanted to be admired as the leader and provider that he was trying so hard to be for the sake of his family.

Most importantly, he wanted a wife who would bring out the best in him – a friend, a companion, a lover, a spiritual partner. Was Sarah really the one for him?

Sarah suddenly pushed open the kitchen door, breaking Ahmad's training of thought. She stumbled in, struggling to hold all the grocery bags in her hands. Ahmad looked over at her.

"Do you want some help?" he asked flatly.

"Ugh…no. It's okay. I've got it." Sarah replied sheepishly.

Whatever. Ahmad thought. *She never accepts my help and then complains how I don't do enough for her. I can't win.*

Ahmad turned around, facing his back to Sarah, and stared outside the window at the children playing. Abdullah was pushing Yasmine on the swing set. Yasmine's curly black hair was flying around with her as she moved up to the sky and back down to the ground. She gleefully laughed with each push, egging Abdullah on to keep playing with her.

Ahmad smiled. He loved his kids.

"Ummm...ughh...ummm...how are you?" Sarah said, struggling to start a conversation.

"Fine," Ahmad replied without much emotion.

"Oh...ugh...nice...good...ummm..." Sarah said nervously.

Ahmad couldn't be bothered to figure out what was on her mind today. Maybe he should stop caring altogether.

"Would you like some lunch?" Sarah offered in an unusually sweet tone of voice.

"No. I just ate."

"Mmm...ohhh...okay." Sarah blushed. She wasn't acting like her normal confident self.

She stood in the middle of the kitchen staring at Ahmad. He could see her blurred form out of the corner of his eyes. He felt her hesitant state. She was being super weird today.

"You should...I need...ummm..." Sarah stammered.

Ahmad started to mentally prepare himself for an oncoming attack. His defenses began to rise. He wasn't going to put up with her nonsense today. He didn't want to hear about any wrong that he was doing, especially on his day-off.

Sarah took a deep breath. She couldn't believe how hard it was to express her needs to her husband.

"I was going to eat something, and I really wanted you to eat with me," she managed to say in a shy voice.

Ahmad squinted. *What?*

He turned around and found Sarah looking at the floor with an awkward expression all over her face. She appeared embarrassed, like she was asking him out on a date.

Ahmad hesitated. Was this a trick? He was ready for the onslaught. He wasn't going to lose this time.

Sarah raised her gaze and forced a smile. Ahmad felt his defenses go down slightly. She was beautiful when she smiled.

"Okay. I've got ten minutes to spare. Then I need to go out with Muhammad."

Sarah felt a tinge of disappointment. She wanted more time with him. She didn't know what to do. This was all new for her. Was this a good or bad sign? Before today, she would have told him that he never had time for her and she was fed up with it.

"Ummm...sure," Sarah said, trying to be more accommodating.

What's going on with her? Ahmad wondered.

"I picked up some sandwiches at that halal joint on the way home," Sarah said with a grin holding up a fast food bag in her right hand.

"I'm a bit full, but I can find room for more now that you mention it."

Sarah giggled. Ahmad smiled. He liked this type of Sarah. He began to loosen up more.

Sarah tried to find a subject to talk about. It was hard to relate to Ahmad. It was as if she didn't know him anymore. How could that be when they lived together? It was like they were roommates, not lovers.

The two soon found themselves engaging in light small talk, catching up with each other's lives. It felt like a date – only that it was in the middle of their kitchen.

"And then I told my boss that he can't expect Michael to lead the new deal when he was still a rookie. That's when he suggested that I head the project. I was a bit shy to accept but I couldn't let them down." Ahmad paused, secretly hoping for an enthusiastic response.

Sarah was clueless about his innate need for admiration. While Ahmad was talking about work, she couldn't help but compare herself to him. She would have chosen differently in some of the situations he mentioned, especially about taking on another big project.

Maybe if he stopped trying to lead everything, he would spend more time at home; then, they would have a better marriage. It was a logical conclusion. Why couldn't he see it?

Ahmad's heart sunk in her silence. He felt empty again.

"Forget it. I won't talk about work with you," he muttered, promising himself to never show his vulnerability to her again. Sarah's face was expressionless.

"Anyway, like I said, I have to go out with Muhammad." He pushed back his chair and slowly rose from the table, still wishing she would say something positive about his work ethic – that she noticed he was exerting himself for the sake of the family and she appreciated it.

But Sarah was stumped. She wanted him to give her more time. Had ten minutes passed by that quickly?

"Ugh, okay," she said, still unsure with how to respond to what he mentioned about leading a new project without questioning his choices.

Ahmad grabbed the car keys and left in a hurry.

Chapter Nine:

From Roommates To Soulmates

Sarah clutched her cell phone and searched frantically for Aisha's number. She was desperate. She needed advice badly and all doors were closed, except the road to Damascus.

"Assalamu alaykum," Aisha answered in a thick Arabic accent.

"wa alaykum assalam Aisha. It's Sarah...err..."

Sarah's mind went blank. What was she doing? She hardly knew Aisha. How was she supposed to explain what was happening in her marriage? She was married to her brother-in-law. How embarrassing!

Aisha caught on quickly. Coming from a big family, she was greatly in tune with her emotional intelligence. She knew how to read people very well.

"Good to hear your voice Sarah. I can't stop thinking about our conversation the other day. How are things going with you and Ahmad?"

Sarah felt relieved. She didn't know how to bring the subject up of her relationship with Aisha. She thanked Allah that He made it so easy for her.

"Oh, AlhamduliLlah. It's been going fine. I've been thinking about our conversation too. I found your advice really interesting. Ummm... ughh...I know someone who would really benefit from it. I was wondering if I could ask your advice about her situation. Maybe you could say something to help her. I'll pass the message on."

Sarah's face turned red. She couldn't be direct with Aisha. Deep down inside, she was ashamed of her marriage – she was ashamed of herself.

"Sure, inshaAllah. I will try my best to be of service to you and your friend," Aisha said reassuringly, not wanting to blow Sarah's cover.

"Great. I know she will be grateful. So, she's been married for... err...about ten years...ummm...and she has a few children...errr...and her husband works a lot...and ummm...he's always busy...and she can't connect with him...and all they do is talk about their kids... ugh... yeah...and she doesn't know how to tell him how to do things without him blowing up."

Aisha was compelled to tell Sarah that she knew it was her marriage that she was asking about. She wanted Sarah to be upfront with her. It was easier to give advice when you could talk openly, but she sensed that Sarah did not completely trust her yet. She could only imagine how humiliating it must be to admit that you're having trouble in your marriage, especially to someone who personally knew your husband.

"Oh, that's a sad situation, but it's quite common for people to fall into it, you know, especially after children come into the picture. We all have to put in the work to keep up with our intimate friendships with our husbands, just like we make an effort to keep up with our children as they grow. If we don't grow together with our husbands, we'll become roommates instead of soulmates."

Sarah's mouth dropped open. This was strange. This was the exact word she was using in her mind to describe her relationship with Ahmad: roommates. Maybe Allah was sending her a personal message. She listened carefully.

"There are a few things she can try. I suppose the easiest thing to do is to start noticing anything good that he does. You mentioned that she wants to tell him how to do things, but no one likes to be told what to do. Maybe she can exchange ordering him around for praising and appreciating him."

"But why should she praise and appreciate him when he's doing something wrong?" Sarah questioned. She still didn't comprehend Aisha's logic.

Aisha took a deep breath. She silently prayed for help and for Allah to open Sarah's heart.

"Sarah, it's only wrong from her perspective. She's so convinced that her way is right that she cannot see that her approach is wrong, and it's causing her to lose in her relationship with him. She's pushing her husband away; she will eventually lose him if she doesn't change her method of approach.

"It could be that he's working more hours for a good reason. He obviously doesn't see anything wrong with what he's doing; so, he must be motivated to keep making this choice for a reason. People don't continue to do stupid things. Everyone has a good reason for why they do things. Why doesn't she ask him why he does it instead of assuming that she already knows?"

Sarah felt like a ton of bricks hit her. *Ask instead of assume?*

"Wh-what would asking do for her?" Sarah stammered. She felt overwhelmed with all the foreign information that was coming from her newfound marriage counselor.

"It would help her understand the way he thinks. When we understand how our husbands think, how they prioritize their needs, and how they make decisions, we're better able to communicate and connect with them at a more profound level. We stop blaming them for what they do and we begin to accept them for who they are."

Sarah was starting to feel like a rookie at being her husband's lover. Had she really been married to him for eight years and never stopped to ask him why he chose to work more hours instead of spending more time with her?

She automatically assumed that he didn't care about her. No wonder she didn't know him. She was too busy being angry with his choices that she never sincerely listened to why he chose them. But would he be willing to share his inner thoughts with her if she asked?

She needed more persuading. "What if he won't share his feelings with her when she asks him?"

"Well, he's not going to share his feelings. He's going to explain his logic. Men are innately more in touch with their thinking than their feelings.

"Listen, all she has to say is: 'How come working more hours is so important to you?' That's it. But if she asks this question, she needs to give him the opportunity to answer it without interrupting him. He must feel like he has room to speak freely without the worry of her judging him. It's very simple."

It sounded simple. Sarah was willing to try it. Yet, there was one thing still bothering her.

"But what if she doesn't agree with his logic?" Sarah inquired.

"She doesn't have to agree with his choices in order to respect them." Aisha remarked.

Sarah was confused. How could she do one without the other?

Aisha knew that this concept would be difficult for Sarah to grasp.

"It's quite possible for her to listen to him with the intention to learn more about why her husband values working extra hours instead of trying to prove to him how he could better spend his time," Aisha further explained.

"In fact, it may be that after hearing what he says, she's satisfied with his response and her respect for his way of thinking grows. However, if it's the case that she does not agree with him, she still has a few options."

Sarah gripped the phone tightly to her ear and listened intensely. This was the part of Aisha's advice that mattered to her the most: *What do you do if you do not agree with your husband's choices? How do you still respect them?*

"For one, she can accept that he is choosing to do differently because he is different from her and it's nothing personal. I'm sure he is making his life decisions based on what he believes is best for himself and the family. She can decide to see him for his noble intention. Every human being on this earth craves to be seen for who they are and not what others think they should be. Our husbands are no different, Sarah. Actually, even more so, they want their wives to see them for who they truly are, what values they stand for, and be admired for their ambitions."

Sarah felt weak. Her original doubts about Aisha's concepts were beginning to resurface. Was the solution for her marriage problems to just shut up and change everything that she wanted for her husband's sake? She couldn't do that. It sounded like betrayal to her true self.

"Or if she really feels strongly about the issue, she can express her personal needs and wants to him, but in a way that doesn't make his thinking wrong. I mean it's obvious that she feels threatened by him working so much, but that's usually an indication that there is an unmet personal need or desire on her side.

"If she can tap into what she really wants, turn it into an expression of desire, and voice it to him – cluing him in on what she prefers or needs – she will probably get what she wants from him inshaAllah. Like I said before, it's how she delivers her love script that will inspire him to react or demotivate him from even trying to please her."

"Mmmm...." Sarah replied in a thoughtful tone. "Jazak Allah khayran Aisha. I'll let this sister know and if you don't mind, I'll be in touch with you about her?"

"Sure, inshaAllah," Aisha said coolly. She was keen to play along with Sarah in order to help her.

"AlhamduliLlah. Assalamu alaykum sister."

"wa alakum assalam wa rahmatuLlahi wa barakatuhu *ukhti*"

Sarah hung up the phone and began to set out her action plan.

Chapter Ten:

Round Two

Sarah pushed a sparkling purple headband along her black, long hair. She carefully applied blush to her cheeks and colored her lips with red lipstick. She took a few steps backwards to see her reflection in the mirror.

When was the last time she did this? She felt great. It was two kids and a few gray hairs later, but she still looked youthful. Her top hugged her curves and her flowing skirt added a flare to her outfit.

She heard Ahmad's car pull up to the driveway. Her heart began to beat. She felt butterflies in her stomach. Why was she so nervous? This was her husband.

She carefully walked down the stairs, praying to herself each step along the way. This was it. She was completely determined to make her marriage successful.

Sarah reached the bottom of the stairs as Ahmad flung open the front door.

"Assalamu alaykum," he said as he walked into the house. He peered around to see who was home.

His eyes slowly worked their way over to Sarah. They widened in shock.

"Sarah?" Ahmad said in a startled voice, completely caught aback by her beautiful appearance.

Sarah blushed and timidly smiled.

All of a sudden, Abdullah came running out into the living room.

"Daddddyyyyyyyy!!!!!!!!!!!!!!" He ran into his father's legs, trying to knock him over.

Ahmad pretended that he had been hit hard by the oncoming collision and bent forwards. He then grabbed Abdullah and tickled him. The two of them began to hysterically laugh.

Abdullah looked over at his mother. His eyes lit up with delight and he yelled, "Mommy's become a princess!"

Ahmad and Sarah laughed.

"A princess in our house!!!"

"Shhh, Abdullah. Yasmine's sleeping, and you need to go to bed now too," Sarah said in a strict tone.

"But I'm not tired!" Abdullah pleaded. "I want to play with daddy."

Ahmad quickly glanced over Sarah. She looked stunning.

"Sorry little guy. We'll have to play tomorrow, okay? Daddy has until midnight with the princess until the grand ball is over."

Sarah noticed that Abdullah's face was filled with confusion, but she was growing impatient. She grabbed his little hand and led him down the hall to his bedroom.

"Can I go to the grand ball tomorrow Mommy?" Ahmad heard Abdullah asking innocently.

"Sure inshaAllah," Sarah replied with a smile.

Sarah made her way back into the living room. Ahmad was sitting on the couch waiting for her. He stood up and invited her to sit next to him. Their skin touched. Sarah's heart leapt. She could feel his arm muscles.

Ahmad cut to the chase.

"What's going on with you these days? You're different."

Was that a good thing? Sarah wondered.

"Yeah, I've just been doing some thinking and I've reached a point where I want to do whatever it takes to make our marriage work." She nervously stared into Ahmad's eyes. She had never been so direct with him about her desire to have a good marriage.

Ahmad's mouth dropped open slightly. He immediately tried to mask the shock written all over his face. He didn't want to ruin the mood. He also half-believed what she was saying. Was this a dream?

"AlhamduliLlah," he said. He was speechless. He didn't know how to react. He decided to allow Sarah to take the lead. He was willing to go anywhere she took him when she behaved like this.

"It's been on my mind for quite some time. I did have my doubts, but now I'm more than sure that I want to be in this relationship..." Sarah hesitated. She was scared to say the open truth. "...with you."

Ahmad took a few moments to digest her comment. It eased him to know that she wanted to stay with him, but he needed to be real with her.

"I want to be with you too Sarah, but I want to be straight up. I'm stressed out at work. I need to be with someone who is going to have my back when I come home. I don't want to return home to a wife who criticizes me for how I do things. Do you think that you could stop doing that?"

Sarah's eyes stung with tears. His words hurt her so badly. He was being a bit too honest with her.

Yet, she knew that she was doing it again – trying to control his reaction. But in her mind, she imagined that Ahmad would be the charming prince who whirled her around at the ball and told her that she had never done anything wrong to him – that it was him who was to blame for their problems.

"I'm sorry that I upset you with my comments." Sarah replied, regretting how much she had misunderstood him. "Yes, I am willing to try, but I need something from you too." Her heart was pounding. This wasn't as simple as she thought.

Ahmad sat silently in a curious state.

"You need to…ugh…no…I…"

Ahmad felt his defenses rising again.

"I want you to spend more time with us and less time at work," Sarah blurted out, although it sounded more like an order than a request.

"That's difficult considering that I'm in charge of two teams now," Ahmad shot back.

Sarah sensed his anger. She was making the same mistake again. He wasn't feeling supported. She tried to remember Aisha's words.

When we understand how our husbands think, how they prioritize their needs, and how they make decisions, we're better able to communicate and connect with them at a more profound level. We stop blaming them for what they do and we begin to accept them for who they are.

"How come that's so important to you?" Sarah questioned.

"How come what is important to me?" Ahmad responded, seeking clarification.

"You know…working so much and taking on two teams."

Ahmad remained silent for what seemed like several torturous minutes. He had a thoughtful expression on his face. He was seriously considering her question and was deciding how best to answer.

He finally spoke. "It gives me fulfillment. When I know that I can provide for you and the kids because of my work, I am driven with a purpose."

Sarah sat back and glanced up at the ceiling. She didn't expect that type of answer. How could writing website codes give him fulfillment? For Sarah, spending time with her children was what provided fulfillment.

"Oh…is it working with others? Is that what makes you feel fulfilled?" Sarah inquired further, trying to relate to him in the way that she lived her life.

"No. I don't care if I work with anyone. It's getting a job done and doing it well that gives me fulfillment," Ahmad explained.

"Hmmm…oh…okay. That's interesting. I'm glad I heard your side…umm…" She was stuck again. She couldn't fully grasp what he was saying. It was completely contrary to what drove her to do things.

She didn't know what else to say. She remembered Aisha's story of her sister – that she praised and appreciated her husband.

"And thanks. You're doing great," she quickly added.

Ahmad's heart skipped. This is what he longed to hear from her. This was the way to his heart.

"It's nothing," Ahmad said, brushing off her comment, although he was secretly pleased. "Why are you asking?"

"Ummm...well...it's important to me that we spend more time together as a family, but if that's not as important to you, I don't know what else to do. Maybe we're just different?" she suggested.

"I don't think we're different at all. I love spending time with my kids. Watching them play and grow up is one of my favorite parts about life."

"Really?" Sarah replied, a bit stunned. "But why do you work so much? Wouldn't it be better to spend more time with the kids instead of taking on new projects? They are growing up very quickly. What do you think about that?"

Ahmad paused. "You know I never thought about it that way. I've just been thinking about what I need to provide for them, like a university education."

"Well, providing your time and love is also necessary. I know they crave your presence around them. I really enjoy seeing you spend time with them too. I need to see that more. It's all I want."

"Mmmm…" Ahmad pondered to himself. "Let me think it over. Maybe I can find a way to give them some more time on the weekdays."

Sarah's heart filled with joy. Was this really happening?

"Thank you. That would be great," she said with a half-smile, wondering what Aisha would think of her approach.

She was beginning to feel comfortable with this way of speaking. It was more direct, honest, and polite.

It now dawned on her that she didn't have to change her views or opinions for Ahmad's sake. She merely needed to learn how to express them in an effective way – a way that would connect Ahmad and her together, not draw them apart. Sort of like a love script.

She broke out of her daze and looked over at Ahmad. He was watching her as she contemplated.

"What?" she asked, slightly embarrassed for zoning out in the middle of their conversation.

"I like it when you're reflective."

He leant over and kissed her lips.

"And you look beautiful. Definitely like a princess."

***

Coach's Analysis

Sarah and Ahmad's situation clearly demonstrates what can happen when a couple is not connected.

Each person misunderstands the other person's intentions, speech, and actions.

As a result, they often find themselves butting heads over issues due to these misinterpretations, which will leave each feeling unfilled in their relationship and lonely.

The solution is to learn how to communicate with each other in a way that creates emotional safety and openness.

Sarah's situation specifically highlights several common mistakes that women fall into when trying to communicate with their husbands, all of which will impact the strength of their love connection.

Mistake #1: Listening to bad thoughts instead of keeping a good opinion.

What many people fail to realize is that most marriage problems are actually first born from what is occurring in your mind.

Your thoughts play a huge role in forming your perspective about people, and your judgement will shape the way that you react and respond to others, including your husband.

Feeling upset about your marriage very much boils down to your perspective and your attitude – how you interpret the events occurring in your relationship.

By paying more attention to what you think is right or how things should be instead of trying to understand and empathize with your husband's circumstances, the door to a deeper connection is closed.

Mistake #2: Hiding her true needs and wants from her husband.

One of the biggest and most harmful misconceptions about how to be a successful Muslim wife is that she should not voice her wants or needs because it may annoy her husband. This is an erroneous assumption.

Rather, when a man is told how to earn his wife's satisfaction – and in a way that inspires him – he will feel motivated to provide, protect, and please.

Ahmad was absolutely clueless about Sarah's need to take a break as a housewife, enjoy a night alone with her husband, and see him more involved with the kids' lives.

We could blame Ahmad for being so blind to all of the hints that Sarah was dropping, but who has the telepathic capability to read someone else's mind?

Furthermore, when there is no connection, the other person will never pick up on subtleties.

Yes, it is possible for a man to gain the ability to read his wife to a certain extent, but this doesn't happen by chance.

It usually occurs after she's taught him what are her preferences, boundaries, and needs by way of successful communication.

Mistake #3: Caring more about doing it her way than working towards a solution which accommodates her husband's different perspective.

It's normal and expected in any romantic relationship that each person will have a different definition of love, a different way of living life, a different preference in routine, and a different outlook on how things should be organized and run.

Differences can add richness, depth, and texture to your marriage. If you seek the advantage in them, they can help you grow spiritually, emotionally, and mentally.

In fact, your husband's differences can potentially improve you and vice versa. Often enough, his strengths are your weaknesses and his weaknesses are your strengths.

Your differences are not deficiencies. If you were both the same, you'd have the same blind spots and the same vulnerabilities.

When problems occur, you'd have the same solutions and you probably wouldn't resolve as much as you think you would. Your husband's differences and your differences make you that unique pair.

Some wives keep a negative attitude towards their husbands' differences. It persuades them to waste much of their energy and time on trying to change their husbands so that he can be just like them, which often backfires.

Instead of working with their husbands and growing together as a team, they fight against the tide.

The truth is that even happy couples have loads of differences, but the secret to success is that they adopt a positive attitude towards them.

They accept one another as is and use each other's strengths where they are needed – no matter how foreign their perks may seem.

Thus, the solution isn't in a wife altering her personality, likes, or dislikes. Rather, it rests in learning how to deliver the script – her personalized love script – to her husband.

Women possess a natural skill at uniting people's hearts and drawing others closer to them. With certain words, a wife can easily do the same with her husband.

Can you relate to Sarah's story?

Are you longing for your marriage to change?

Not sure how to start?

Check out "**Say It With Love: Communicate, Connect & Cure Conflict**" at the Muslima Coaching bookstore for wife tips on:

- discovering how to express personal wants/needs in a way that motivates a man to move,
- understanding how to act and react within conflict,
- and knowing how to unlock a man's heart with admiration, appreciation, and much more.

Please review and rate this book! Jazak Allah khayran!

About the Author

Naielah Ackbarali is the **founder** and **CEO** of Muslima Coaching.

She was born in Port of Spain, Trinidad and moved to South Florida in her childhood. She obtained her BA degree from Florida State University with a double major in International Affairs and Sociology. In her early twenties, she moved to Amman, Jordan to study classical Arabic.

Naielah is a trained **wife coach**, certified **life coach**, and a certified **NLP Master Practitioner**. She has written several books on marriage, and she has produced free video courses related to fasting and umrah for ladies.

In her free time, Naielah teaches Hanafi fiqh for women, actively reads self-help and marriage books, and practices developing her cooking/baking skills.

Find her at: http://www.muslimacoaching.com

Other Books By Naielah Ackbarali

HALAL NOVELS & INSPIRATION:

- *"Love Scripts – Getting Through To Him"* for all sisters.

- *"Secrets Of Successful Muslim Wives"* for all married sisters.

WIFE TIPS GUIDES:

- *"Say It With Love: Communicate, Connect & Cure Conflict"* for all married sisters.

- *"Newlywed Nuggets: Golden Marriage Advice"* for newlywed wives.

- *"Finding Your Other Half: 8-Step Action Plan"* for single sisters.

- *"Ten Tips For Dealing With Muslim In-Laws"* for all married sisters.

QUIZ SETS & WORKBOOKS:

- *"Love Connection Kit"* Relationship Quizzes for all married sisters.

Find them at the Muslima Coaching Bookstore, Kindle or Amazon! Please rate and review our books!

About Muslima Coaching

Muslima Coaching is a coaching service that aims to encourage Muslim women to be the best wives, mothers, friends, and daughters that they can be. We coach single women, married women, divorced women, and teenagers (17+).

We offer:

Relationship Coaching – marriage advice centered around traditional Islamic teachings, modern-day marital advice, and self-help tactics for singles, newlyweds, and any married woman

Life Coaching – life guidance geared towards getting in touch with your Islamic purpose/fitra and forming life goals

Emotion Coaching – educational tactics used to teach women how to process, deal with, and react to negative emotional states

Adult Teen Coaching – practical advice of how to transition from a teenager into an adult woman (must be 17+)

Deen Coaching – teaching the rulings related to the five pillars of Islam

Islamic Inspiration – solutions that are built upon and around the deen inshaAllah

Affordable Prices – more than half the price of other coaching services

Group Sessions – courses and workshops teaching sisters about marriage, life, and self-development

Individual Consultation Sessions – unique personal sessions catered to your life circumstances

Complete Confidentiality – no one will know your stuff except us

FREE Video Courses

Umrah For Women

- www.muslimacoaching.com/umra-for-women/

Fasting For Women

- www.muslimacoaching.com/fasting-for-women/

FREE Audio Series

Be His Khadija

- www.muslimacoaching.com/be-his-khadija-audio-series/

Client Testimonials

"I want to tell you how impressive your coaching site is. Women are very blessed to have you. Your positive and uplifting advice is superb. Really valuable stuff!"

"The service you offer is excellent mashallah and is of great value."

"I just finished reading the blog post today and I was so amazed at how beautiful, simple, and wise your advice is. I think any sensitive woman that's been married for more than a few years can attest to its truths. MashaAllah la quwatta illa billah. And I was so awestruck, and I kept thinking how needed and valuable this information is, and I doubt that there is anything similar on the web."

"I just wanted to express my heartfelt gratitude to you for starting and maintaining this website. May Allah reward you and give you barakah in it. I love the fact that the advice here comes from the perspective of religion, from a desire to please Allah subhanahu wa tala in marriage, and at the same time takes into account and directly addresses the

challenges we face in our times. Also, there is great comfort in having the coaching option available for people who might need it."

"I have honestly had such a different outlook since the session alhamduLillah. I have had less stress and worry as I always have and just felt more free than I have with regards to myself. I can't tell you enough what the one-on-one session and the marriage classes have done for me. I'm almost like a new person. It is like I had blinkers on my eyes and by the grace of Allah swt was helped to remove them and see the blessings Allah swt has so generously bestowed upon me. I'm sure if you asked my husband he could vouch for how much I've changed."

"All marriages need work and Muslima Coaching gives great advice for any woman wanting to improve and maintain a good marriage and home."

"I had just accepted that my marriage was the way it was, and there was nothing I could do about it, so I forced myself to be happy and live with it. Now I know there are a list of things I can improve on to get a better marriage! And I feel like I have hope now, alhamdulillah. All the practical advice given

on different situations are like wow, subhanAllah, is it really just as simple as that! Why did I make it so hard for myself all those years!"

"Now step by step I have the keys to open the doors to a beautiful life with my husband and children. Muslima Coaching has helped me to understand my husband and my role as a woman and wife and has thus cleared all my misconceptions of what marriage is. Every woman needs to do this course, I have learnt so much!"

Please Visit Our Site:

www.muslimacoaching.com

53760989R00052

Made in the
USA
Lexington, KY